REAL WORLD DATA

GRAPHING CRIME

Barbara Somervill

Heinemann
LIBRARY

www.heinemannlibrary.co.uk
Visit our website to find out more information about Heinemann Library books.

To order:
☎ Phone +44 (0) 1865 888066
🖹 Fax +44 (0) 1865 314091
💻 Visit www.heinemannlibrary.co.uk

Heinemann Library is an imprint of Capstone Global Library Limited, a company incorporated in England and Wales having its registered office at 7 Pilgrim Street, London, EC4V 6LB – Registered company number: 6695582

"Heinemann" is a registered trademark of Pearson Education Limited, under licence to Capstone Global Library Limited

Edited by Megan Cotugno and Diyan Leake
Designed by Victoria Bevan and Geoff Ward
Original illustrations © Capstone Global Library Ltd 2010
Illustrated by Geoff Ward
Picture research by Ruth Blair, Zooid Pictures Ltd
Originated by Chroma Graphics (Overseas) Pte Ltd
Printed in China by Leo Paper Products Ltd

ISBN 978 0 431033 40 2 (hardback)
14 13 12 11 10
10 9 8 7 6 5 4 3 2 1

British Library Cataloguing in Publication Data
Somervill, Barbara A.
Graphing crime. – (Real world data)
364'.0728-dc22
A full catalogue record for this book is available from the British Library.

Acknowledgements
We would like to thank the following for permission to reproduce photographs: Alamy pp. **18** (© Design Pics Inc.), **23** (© Peter Jordan); Corbis pp. **8** (William Whitehurst, **24** (Guy Cali), **26** (Scott Houston); Getty Images pp. **4** (Yu)ri Contez/AFP), **10** (Phil Walter), **16** (Indranil Mukherjee/AFP); © Interpol p. **22**; PA Photos p. **14** (Associated Press); Photolibrary p. **12**; Rex Features p. **6** (Sipa Press); Shutterstock p. **20** (kenny1).

Cover photograph of a cell in old Ohio State Reformatory, USA reproduced with permission of Getty Images (Altrendo Travel).

Every effort has been made to contact copyright holders of any material reproduced in this book. Any omissions will be rectified in subsequent printings if notice is given to the publisher.

Disclaimer
All the Internet addresses (URLs) given in this book were valid at the time of going to press. However, due to the dynamic nature of the Internet, some addresses may have changed, or sites may have changed or ceased to exist since publication. While the author and publishers regret any inconvenience this may cause readers, no responsibility for any such changes can be accepted by either the author or the publishers.

CONTENTS

Some words are printed in bold, **like this**. You can find out what they mean by looking in the glossary, on page 30.

Crime is the act of doing something that is against the law. Every country has government officials that make its laws. Lawmakers also decide which crimes are the most serious and what **punishments** people get for breaking laws. Governments employ police to **enforce** laws. If a law is broken and a person is charged with committing a crime, judges, a legal team, and juries work to find out if a person is **guilty** or **innocent**. Because nations make their own laws, what is considered a crime – and the punishments handed out – can be different from country to country.

Graphing crime

This book uses graphs to show information about crime. Graphs are a way to show information visually. There are many different types of graphs, but all graphs make it easier to see patterns quickly. You can see patterns in crime in the graphs shown in this book.

 When the police capture a suspected criminal, they record that person's fingerprints.

International or national?

Most crimes only affect people within the country in which they occur. These crimes, such as **murder** and bank robbery, are handled by police and **courts** in that country.

Other crimes can be **international** crimes. This means the crimes take place in several countries, or the **criminals** move goods or money from one country to another. Drug **trafficking** is an international crime, one which requires the co-operation of police in many countries.

Crime around the world

The table below shows the number of reported crimes for every 1,000 people in nine countries for the years 1998–2000. The bar graph shows the same information in graph form. By showing the statistics in visual form, the chart allows the reader to quickly compare the crime rates for each country.

Country	Reported crimes per 1,000 population	Country	Reported crimes per 1,000 population
India	1.6	United States	80
Turkey	4.1	United Kingdom	85.5
Mexico	12.8	Denmark	92.8
Japan	19.2	Dominica	113.8
France	62.1		

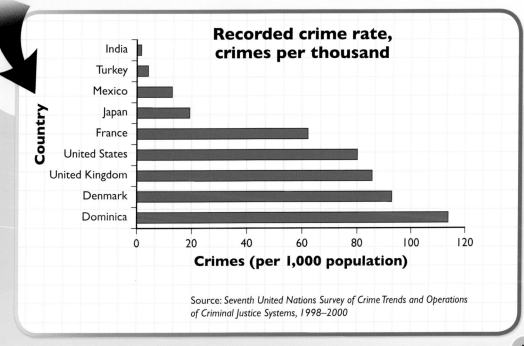

Source: Seventh United Nations Survey of Crime Trends and Operations of Criminal Justice Systems, 1998–2000

CATEGORIES OF CRIMES

Crimes can be divided into several groups. Some countries, such as the United Kingdom and other Commonwealth countries, divide crimes into **summary** offences (minor crimes) and serious crimes. Other countries, including the United States, divide crimes into **misdemeanours** (minor crimes) and **felonies** (serious crimes). In some countries, for serious crimes, a **grand jury** decides if there is enough **evidence** to charge a person with a felony. All nations agree that murder, **arson**, kidnapping, and drug trafficking are serious crimes.

 Starting a fire on purpose is called arson. Arson is a serious crime that costs millions of pounds every year.

Victims of crime

Another way to categorize crimes is by looking at the **victims** of crimes. Crimes against people are usually serious crimes. Such crimes include **assault**, robbery, kidnapping, and murder. The victims of these crimes have been harmed directly, or even killed.

Crimes against property deal with damage to or taking things owned by people, businesses, or the public. These crimes include breaking and entering, burglary, vandalism, and arson. Burglars steal from a home or business when no people are there. Robbers take money directly from people. So robbery is a felony as well as a crime against property.

Crimes against a government are crimes against all the citizens of a nation. **Terrorism** is a crime against a government. So is killing a public official. A common crime against a government is counterfeiting, which is printing and using fake money.

People everywhere commit minor crimes. They are not considered criminals. Speeding and parking illegally are summary offences. People found guilty of summary usually pay fines or do **community service** if they are found guilty.

Crime rates in England and Wales, 1981 and 2006–07

Pie charts show parts of a whole. The two pie charts below compare crimes committed in England and Wales in 1981 and in 2006–07. The percentages of crimes did not change much over 25 years. (The crimes listed on the key do not include every type of crime that happened in England and Wales. These were crimes tracked for this particular report.)

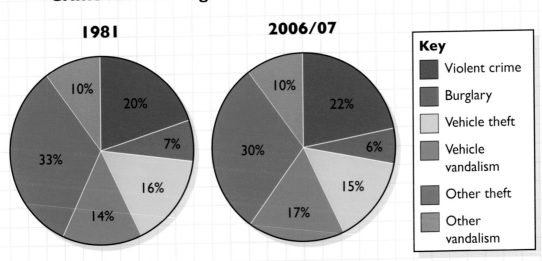

Crime rates in England and Wales, 1981 and 2006/07

1981 — 10%, 20%, 7%, 16%, 14%, 33%

2006/07 — 10%, 22%, 6%, 15%, 17%, 30%

Key
- Violent crime
- Burglary
- Vehicle theft
- Vehicle vandalism
- Other theft
- Other vandalism

Source: *Crime in England and Wales, 2006/7* by the British Home Office

MURDER

The official word for taking another person's life is **homicide**. Under the law, there can be several different levels of homicide. The differences among types of homicide change from nation to nation.

Types of murder

Premeditated murder is a planned killing. It is not a killing committed in a sudden fit of anger. The murderer decides to commit the murder, works out how to do it, and kills someone. In some countries, criminals who commit premeditated murder may be put to death for their crimes. In other countries, murderers go to **prison**.

Vehicular homicide or vehicular **manslaughter** happens when a person kills another with a car, lorry, or motorcycle. In this type of murder, the weapon is the car or lorry. **Hit-and-run** deaths and deaths that are caused by drunk drivers are examples of vehicular manslaughter.

Manslaughter is causing a death by accident. The line between manslaughter and accidental death can be hard to understand. Manslaughter includes being reckless or foolish, or acting when angry. An example of manslaughter would be two men getting into a fight, and one killing the other by hitting the victim with a bat.

 When the police investigate a homicide, they mark the place where the body was found.

Who commits murder?

Globally, more adult men commit homicide than women. In most developed countries, men commit seven to ten times as many murders as women. Children can also commit homicide, and the number of child murderers is growing. Homicide victims range from infants to senior citizens, family members to strangers.

High murder rate, or just high population?

Some charts can be misleading. The pie chart below shows that India has a large number of total reported murders. However, as the table reveals, India's murder rate is low when its large population is taken into account.

Country	Murders reported per 100,000 people	Country	Murders reported per 100,000 people
Colombia	61.7	Ukraine	9.4
South Africa	49.6	Thailand	8.0
Venezuela	31.6	Philippines	7.8
Russia	20.2	United States	4.3
Mexico	13.0	India	3.4

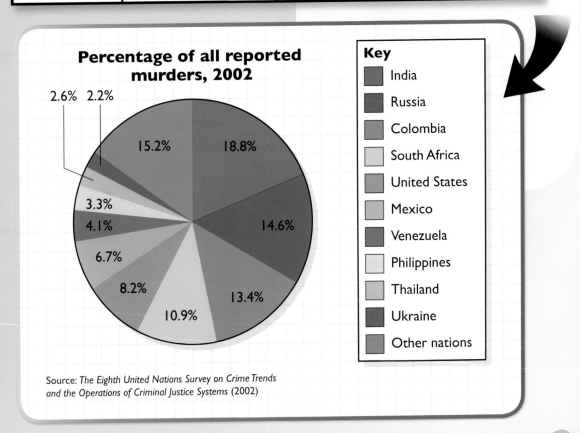

Percentage of all reported murders, 2002

2.6% 2.2%
15.2%
18.8%
3.3%
4.1%
14.6%
6.7%
8.2%
13.4%
10.9%

Key
- India
- Russia
- Colombia
- South Africa
- United States
- Mexico
- Venezuela
- Philippines
- Thailand
- Ukraine
- Other nations

Source: *The Eighth United Nations Survey on Crime Trends and the Operations of Criminal Justice Systems* (2002)

ORGANIZED CRIME

Organized crime is an international problem. An organized crime gang is run like a military organization. Like an army, organized crime gangs have ranks of soldiers. The head of a crime group is the group's general. The head gives orders to officers, who pass the orders down to street soldiers. Organized crime is involved in drug trafficking, immigration crimes, gambling, and **money laundering**.

Drugs

Drug trafficking covers several different crimes, from growing or making drugs, to shipping them around the world and selling them on street corners. Such activities are **illegal** in most countries. But there is a lot of money to be made, which is why so many criminals are involved in drug trafficking.

 Drug trafficking is a huge problem around the world. This photo shows confiscated drugs, weapons, and money.

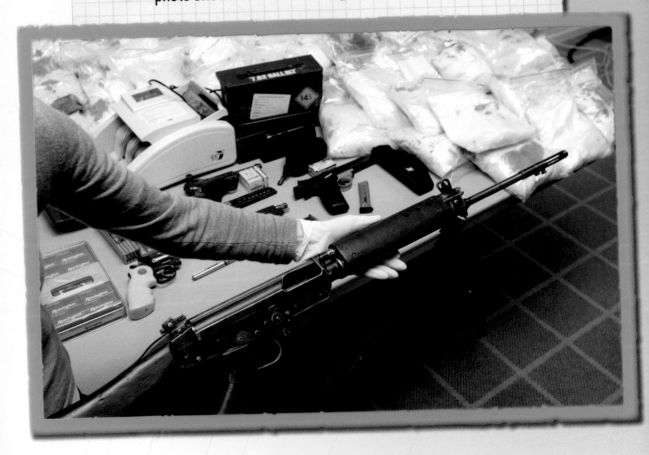

People

Organized crime also traffics in people. When people want to move to a new country and are not allowed to do so, they may pay someone to sneak them into the new country. This is immigration crime. Like drug trafficking, immigration crime needs an army of workers to be a success.

Money

Gambling can be a way of cheating people out of money. Organized crime is involved in many types of gambling. Criminals run casinos and collect sports and horse-racing bets. Gamblers may win once in a while, but the real winners in organized crime gambling operations are the criminals.

Money earned in illegal ways is called dirty money. The money can be traced to crime. Criminals do not want to be caught with dirty money, arrested, and convicted, so they launder it. Money laundering "cleans" dirty money. Criminals **invest** dirty money in legal companies and real estate. They sell what they buy and put the money in a different bank. They send the money through many banks and accounts. The banks do not tell who owns the accounts, so law officers cannot trace the money. When money laundering is complete, criminals spend the money on things they want.

Following the money

A flow chart shows the steps involved in a process. The first step in this chart is selling drugs. Criminals "clean" the money earnt selling drugs by investing it. They take the profits from their investments and use the "clean" cash.

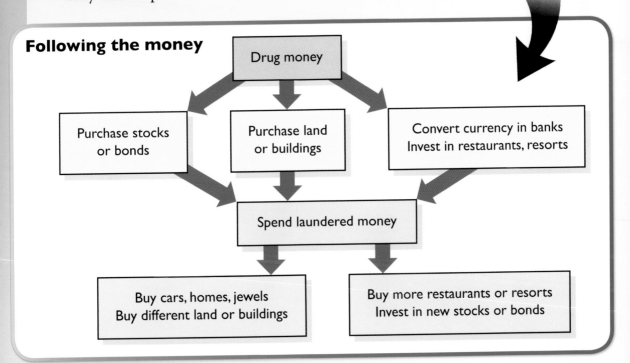

Following the money

Drug money

Purchase stocks or bonds

Purchase land or buildings

Convert currency in banks
Invest in restaurants, resorts

Spend laundered money

Buy cars, homes, jewels
Buy different land or buildings

Buy more restaurants or resorts
Invest in new stocks or bonds

Drug-related crime

Illegal drug use is a problem all over the world. Crimes committed because of drugs are also a worldwide problem. Murder, theft, and violent acts are often linked to drug use. These are drug-related crimes.

The most common illegal drugs are cannabis (marijuana), cocaine, ecstasy, amphetamines, and heroin. Shipping, selling, and buying illegal drugs is called drug trafficking.

Many people also commit crimes because they take drugs. People who use drugs may become desperate to get them. They may mug or rob people to get money to pay for drugs. They may break into businesses and steal money or goods that they sell to buy drugs. Under the power of some drugs, users may become violent. They fight and sometimes murder others.

 Drug use among teenagers is increasing, as are drug-related crimes committed by teenagers.

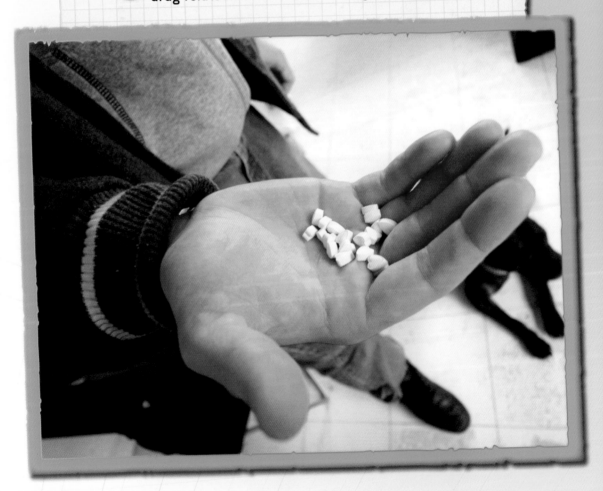

A study by the United Nations shows a growing number of young people involved in drug or alcohol abuse and violent crimes. More male teenagers commit drug-related offences than females. The number of male **offenders** gets higher each year, along with the number of arrests. The number of female offenders also increases, but at a much slower rate than the number of males.

As drug use increases, so do the numbers of drug-related crimes. Illegal drug trafficking is a multi-billion pound business. Enforcing drug laws and dealing with drug-related crimes also costs billions of pounds.

Drug-related crimes in the European Union

This line graph shows the increase in reported drug-related crimes in European Union countries. The graph starts at 100 in order to show the increase more clearly. Although this graph deals only with the European Union, the patterns shown are similar all over the world.

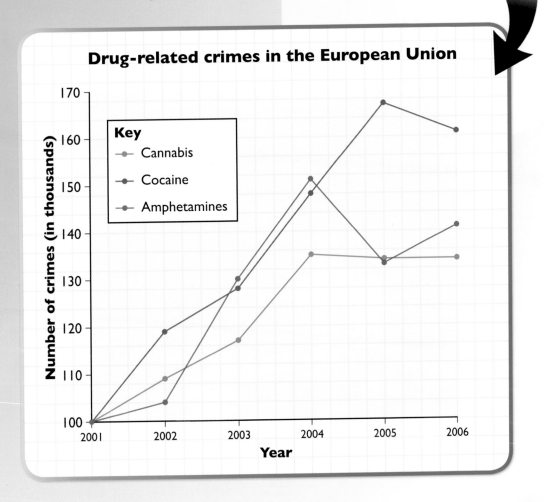

Drug-related crimes in the European Union

HATE CRIMES

Hatred may begin because of differences in race, religion, sex, or a person's sexual interests. Sometimes, hate boils over and leads to crime. Hate crime is increasing all over the world. To try to stop hate crimes from taking place, many nations now give harsh punishments to people who commit them. People who are guilty of committing hate crimes may pay higher fines or serve longer prison **sentences**.

Common victims of hate crimes are people who may seem different. They may be people from foreign countries who have moved into an area. Victims may practise a different religion. Their skin may be a different colour.

Some hate crimes might seem minor. However, it is against the law for a person to write a nasty name on a shop window or make harassing phone calls. Often, minor acts lead to more serious crimes. Hate crime victims regularly suffer injuries and sometimes death.

 In the United States, a group called the Ku Klux Klan committed hate crimes against African Americans from 1865 into the 1960s.

14

Solving the problem

Police departments worldwide have similar goals in dealing with hate crimes. The first goal is to encourage people to report these crimes. In recent years, more people have been reporting hate crimes that may have gone unreported in the past.

Police try to answer hate crime reports quickly and treat victims fairly. They hope that by arresting people who commit hate crimes, it will stop others from committing similar crimes.

Hate crimes on the rise?

This graph shows the rise in reported hate crimes committed from 2006 to 2007. Although the increases for the United Kingdom and United States are low, the number of hate crimes reported was high. There were 61,262 racial hate crimes reported in the UK. In the United States, 7,624 hate crimes were reported. In many countries, the numbers may be rising because these crimes are being reported more often.

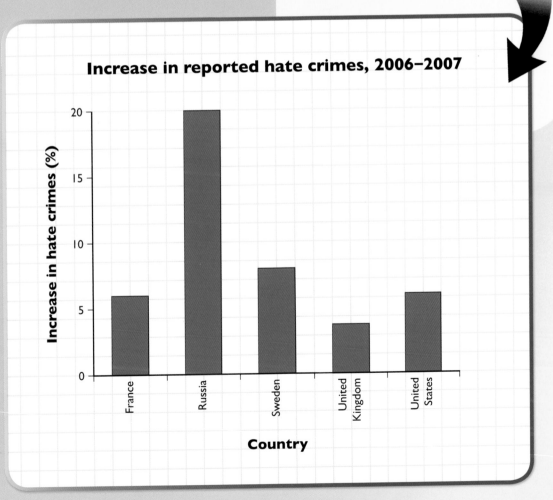

Increase in reported hate crimes, 2006–2007

Terrorism threatens all people. A suicide bomber goes into a restaurant and sets off a bomb. A group kidnaps a news reporter and holds the reporter for ransom. Terrorists hijack two jets and crash them into New York's World Trade Center. Pirates take over a cruise ship, rob the passengers, and kill the crew. Whether an act kills thousands of people or destroys property, these are all acts of terrorism. Terrorists want to make people afraid, and they succeed.

Why?

The reasons for committing terrorist acts are many. Terrorists believe that their actions will support their religion or political views. Some want to put an end to a government or show their hatred of other people.

In 2008, terrorists captured and murdered hostages in Mumbai, India. One of their targets was the Taj Mahal hotel.

Stopping terrorists

All countries have plans to deal with terrorists. Airports have high levels of security. People and luggage are screened to stop terrorists bringing bombs on board. Countries share any information they have about terrorists with other nations. They work together to arrest and convict known terrorists.

INTERPOL, an international police agency, works to end terrorist activities. INTERPOL agents track large shipments of weapons all over the world. They watch activities of known terrorist groups and try to uncover their plans. They let countries know about terrorists' movements and meetings.

The problem with stopping terrorism is working out who is a terrorist. Terrorists often have ordinary jobs. They may be teachers, doctors, plumbers, or secretaries. They may live in ordinary homes with ordinary families. Most terrorists do not act alone. They are part of a **cell**, but each individual may not know who else is in their cell.

Increase in global terrorist attacks

This line graph shows how terrorism has increased around the world. The number of attacks increased from 208 in 2003 to 11,111 in 2005. The number of deaths from terrorist attacks increased from 625 to 14,602 during the same time period. The numbers of incidents and deaths continues to rise. In November 2008, terrorists occupied two hotels in Mumbai, India. These acts of terrorism were shown in television news reports around the world.

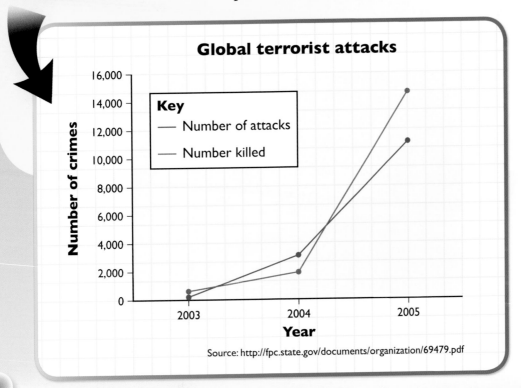

Global terrorist attacks

Key
— Number of attacks
— Number killed

Number of crimes

Year

Source: http://fpc.state.gov/documents/organization/69479.pdf

WHITE-COLLAR CRIMES: FRAUD

People who commit **white-collar** crimes may not look like criminals. "White collar" refers to jobs where people wear white shirts and suits. People who carry out these crimes do not carry guns or knives. They do not sell drugs. Most white-collar criminals commit their crimes at work. White-collar crimes are mostly related to money.

White-collar **fraud** includes writing cheques that will bounce, stealing and using another person's **identification**, and selling goods or services that do not exist. Criminals use these acts to steal money from their victims.

Fraud can also involve stealing from a company. Often, the thief works in the company and uses his or her job to take the money. That is called embezzlement. Another form of fraud is insurance fraud. People fake accidents or burn buildings so they can collect insurance money.

 With a fake driver's licence or identification, criminals can get credit information which they can use to steal money.

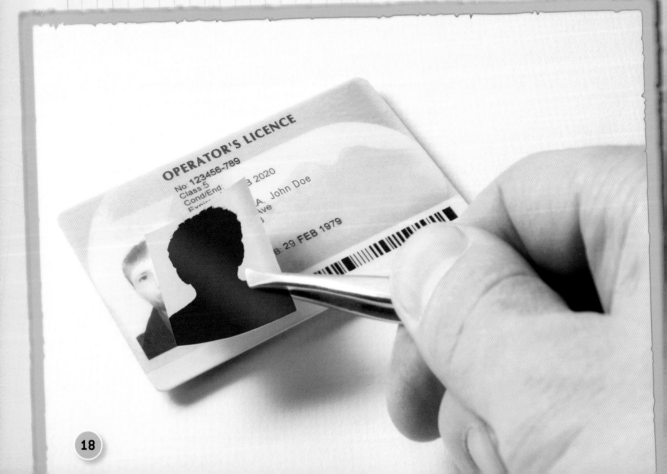

Fraud and the Internet

With the growth of the Internet, fraud has become a global crime. Fraud can be committed anywhere in the world against anyone else in the world. A common Internet fraud is sending an email saying that a person has won money in a contest. "Send your name, bank account number, and other identification information," says the email. "We will put your winnings in the bank." Fraudsters use the information they collect to take money from their victims' bank accounts or run up credit card bills in the name of their victims. Criminals steal millions of pounds each year through Internet crime.

According to the Federal Bureau of Investigation (FBI), 66 per cent of cyber (Internet) fraud begins in the United States. The UK accounts for 10.5 per cent of cyber fraud, followed by Nigeria with 7.5 per cent, and Canada with 3 per cent.

Top 10 Internet scams, 2007

The pie chart shows the 10 most common Internet scams from around the world in 2007. The data is based on the number of complaints made to police during that year.

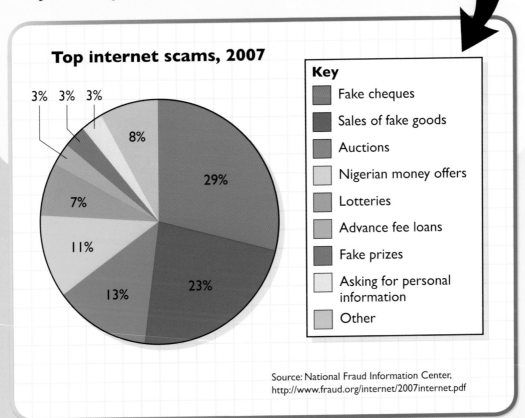

Top internet scams, 2007

3% 3% 3%
8%
29%
7%
11%
13%
23%

Key
- Fake cheques
- Sales of fake goods
- Auctions
- Nigerian money offers
- Lotteries
- Advance fee loans
- Fake prizes
- Asking for personal information
- Other

Source: National Fraud Information Center, http://www.fraud.org/internet/2007internet.pdf

Juvenile offenders are young people who have been arrested for crimes. The age that is considered juvenile varies from place to place, but it is usually up to around the age of 17. Juvenile offenders usually commit property crimes. They destroy property, shoplift, or light fires. Juvenile offenders most often commit crimes with friends. Some juvenile offenders feel pushed into crime by their friends.

Many juvenile crimes are not reported or no arrests are made. Juvenile offenders are more likely to be caught committing crimes, but they are also more likely to be bailed out by their parents. Some first-time offenders are let go with a warning. Overall, juvenile crimes that are reported may be only a fraction of the crimes that are really committed.

The rise of gangs

Gang membership has increased, and gang presence is spreading. Gangs were once only found in cities. Now, small towns and rural communities report gang activities. Many gang-related crimes are not reported. People fear other gang members will hurt them if they call the police.

Gang members usually wear special clothing and sometimes have tattoos. The "gang look" shows who belongs to the gang, and may frighten other people. Children and teenagers who wear gang-like clothing put themselves in danger. In recent years, gangs have killed children simply for wearing gang-related clothing.

Alleys like this one can become a gang's territory – and a very dangerous place.

Percentage of UK juvenile offenders who committed various crimes	
Juveniles who attended school	**Juveniles who did not attend school**
Fare-skipping: 46%	Handling stolen goods: 60%
Graffiti/vandalism: 34%	Assault: 57%
Shoplifting: 33%	Possessing a weapon: 55%
Criminal damage: 29%	Shoplifting: 49%
Possessing a weapon: 29%	Buying drugs: 48%

Juvenile offenders

Children who attend school are less likely to commit serious crimes. As the table above shows, juveniles who attend school are more likely to be caught shoplifting or committing vandalism. Those who are not in school commit crimes such as assault and buying drugs. Male offenders are more likely than females to commit certain crimes, as the chart below of juveniles in the United States shows.

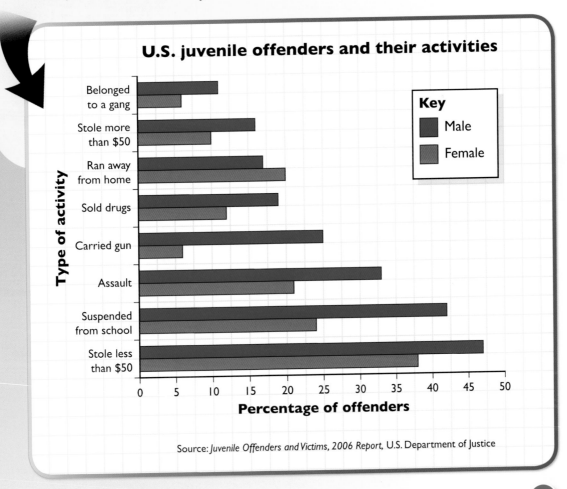

Source: *Juvenile Offenders and Victims, 2006 Report*, U.S. Department of Justice

THE POLICE

Police officers work to stop crime and catch criminals. They answer emergency calls to help people in trouble. Police agencies work in local, national, and international situations.

In a **local police** force, officers control traffic and patrol neighbourhoods. These police officers usually wear uniforms. After a serious crime has been committed, trained police **detectives** try to work out who committed the crime. Detectives are called plain-clothes police because they wear ordinary clothes instead of uniforms.

Today, police work also takes place in laboratories, where officers sift through evidence to help solve crimes. Other police officers keep records and work on computers.

Organization

In the UK, police rankings are standard throughout the country. Police officers rise from constable to sergeant, then inspector, and on up to the most senior position of Chief Constable. Detectives hold separate ranks.

What is INTERPOL?

INTERPOL is the world's largest international police organization, with 187 member countries. It was created in 1923 and allows police organizations in different countries to work together. It also helps all organizations, authorities, and services whose mission is to prevent or fight international crime. INTERPOL's headquarters are in Lyon, France, and there are seven regional offices throughout the rest of the world. There are also Special Representatives at the United Nations in New York, USA and the European Union in Brussels, Belgium. Each member country has a National Central Bureau which is run by national law-enforcement officers.

 The police put dangerous suspects in handcuffs.

Where do most police officers work?

This bar graph shows that the majority of police officers in the United States work for local police departments. This is true for most countries. Local police are the first step in preventing crime.

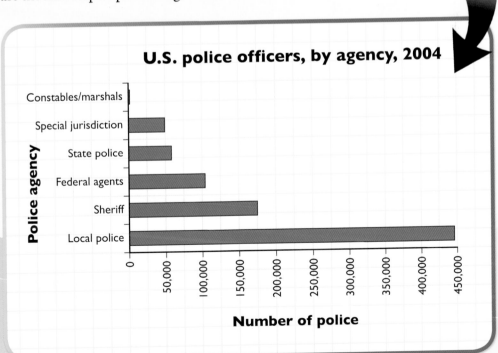

U.S. police officers, by agency, 2004

Most developed nations have court systems that deal with people who are accused of committing a crime. When the police have collected enough evidence to arrest a person, the criminal **justice** system goes into action.

When people are first accused of committing crimes, their pictures and fingerprints are taken. Their cases are given a number, and their personal information is recorded. They sometimes go to prison.

 Witnesses swear to tell the truth. Failing to tell the truth, which is known as perjury, is a serious crime.

On trial

The case is prepared for **trial**. There are two sides in a court trial. The **prosecution** presents the case for the government. The side that speaks for the accused personal is the **defence**. In a trial, the accused person is called the **defendant**.

In the courtroom, the judge controls the trial. The judge makes sure the trial follows the law and the defendant's rights are protected. A **jury** of ordinary people listens to the evidence presented in the trial. When the trial begins, the prosecution presents evidence against the defendant. Witnesses who have evidence about the crime have the chance to speak. They must swear to tell the truth. Both the prosecution and the defence present and question every witness.

Weighing the evidence

After all the evidence is presented, the jury talks about what they learnt. They vote to decide if the defendant is guilty or not guilty. In many cases, all members of a jury must agree in order to find the defendant guilty. A person who is found not guilty goes free. A person who is found guilty does not.

Cases tried at the Crown Court

Summary offences are tried at magistrates' courts. Serious crimes are tried at the **Crown Court**. This pie chart shows the outcomes of Crown Court cases between 2006 and 2007. It illustrates that by far the largest proportion of defendants entered a guilty plea.

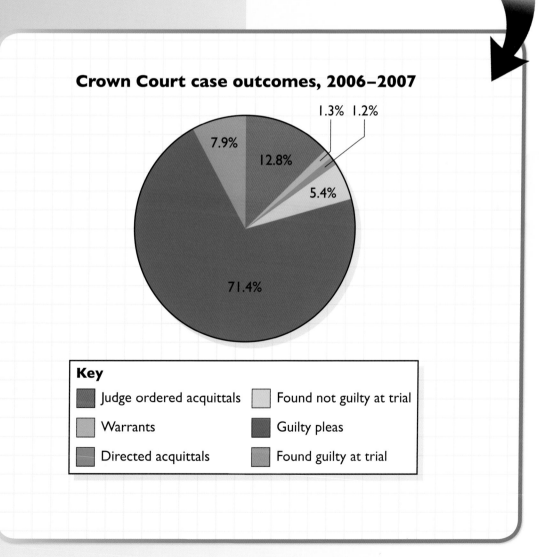

Crown Court case outcomes, 2006–2007

1.3% 1.2%
7.9%
12.8%
5.4%
71.4%

Key

- ■ Judge ordered acquittals
- ■ Warrants
- ■ Directed acquittals
- ■ Found not guilty at trial
- ■ Guilty pleas
- ■ Found guilty at trial

Punishment

Laws require that people who are guilty of crimes pay for what they have done. A judge decides what a guilty person's sentence is, although the law suggests penalties for certain crimes. A guilty person may be sent to prison. The time spent in prison is called a sentence. Other punishments might be fines, community service, or **probation**.

Prison

In prison, convicts live in cells, and their days are controlled. They eat meals, work, and live by a schedule set by the prison. Prisons are rated by how "secure" they are. Minimum-security prisons allow prisoners to work in jobs within the prison and outside. One common job outside the prison is picking up litter along a road. Maximum-security prisons are for seriously dangerous criminals. Prisoners in these prisons have little freedom. They spend most of their time in their cells.

Prison sentences vary from country to country and crime to crime. The table on page 27 shows the penalties for drug trafficking in several countries.

 Prisoners live a very controlled life. They spend most of their time in small cells.

Country	Sentence for conviction of drug trafficking
Brunei, India, Laos, Thailand, North Korea, Singapore, Indonesia, Malaysia	Death penalty
United States	5 to 40 years
United Kingdom	Minimum: 7 years for those convicted 3 times
Austria	1 to 10 years
Denmark	Up to 16 years for class A drugs

Parole

After serving time in prison, a person may be eligible for **parole**. Parole allows a prisoner to leave prison but still be watched. A person on parole must get a job, have a place to live, and stay away from known criminals. People on parole cannot carry weapons. They must check in with their parole officers every month to make sure they are following parole rules.

Like a prison sentence, parole lasts for a certain amount of time.

When prison sentences or parole terms end, convicted people are free. However, they will always have a criminal record. That record follows them throughout their lives.

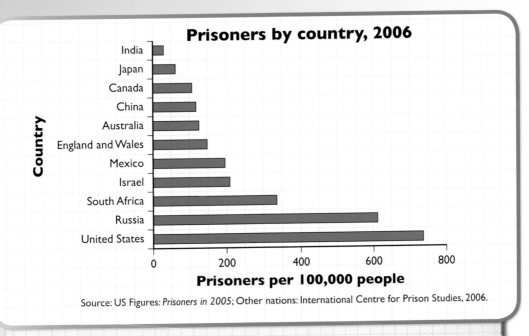

Prisoners by country, 2006

Source: US Figures: *Prisoners in 2005*; Other nations: International Centre for Prison Studies, 2006.

 This bar graph shows the number of prisoners per 100,000 people. In 2006, the United States had the most prisoners, 737 for every 100,000 people, followed by Russia with 611.

CHART SMARTS

Data are bits of information about something. We get data as a list of facts or a mass of numbers. It can be difficult to understand large amounts of data. Graphs and charts are ways of displaying information visually. We can see relationships and patterns in data presented in graphs and charts. The type of chart used depends on the data that needs to be represented.

Pie charts

A pie chart is used to show the different parts of a whole picture. A pie chart is the best way to show how something is divided up. These charts show information as different-sized portions of a circle. They can help you compare proportions. You can easily see which section is the largest "slice" of the pie.

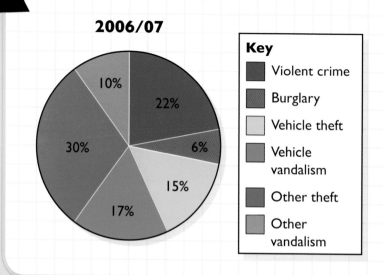

Crime rates in England and Wales

2006/07

10%, 22%, 30%, 6%, 15%, 17%

Key
- Violent crime
- Burglary
- Vehicle theft
- Vehicle vandalism
- Other theft
- Other vandalism

Line graphs

Line graphs use lines to connect points on a graph. They can be used to show how something changes over time. If you put several lines on one line graph, you can compare the overall pattern of several sets of data.

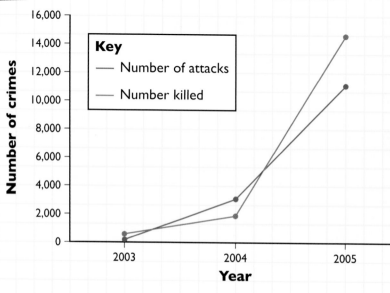

Global terrorist attacks

Number of crimes

16,000
14,000
12,000
10,000
8,000
6,000
4,000
2,000
0

Key
— Number of attacks
— Number killed

2003   2004   2005

Year

Bar graphs

A bar graph is a good way to compare amounts of different things. Bar graphs have a horizontal **x-axis** and a vertical **y-axis**. The x-axis often shows the scale of comparison. The y-axis shows the items being compared.

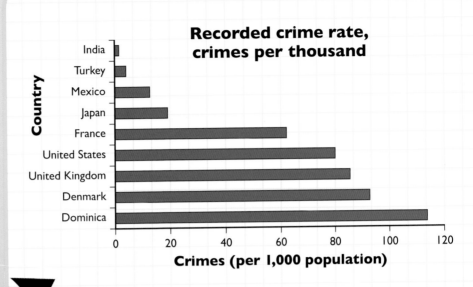

Bar graphs can also compare two sets of data. Both sets of information are based on the same scale and categories of information. This type of graph can be used to compare males and females, similar data from different countries, or data from two different time periods.

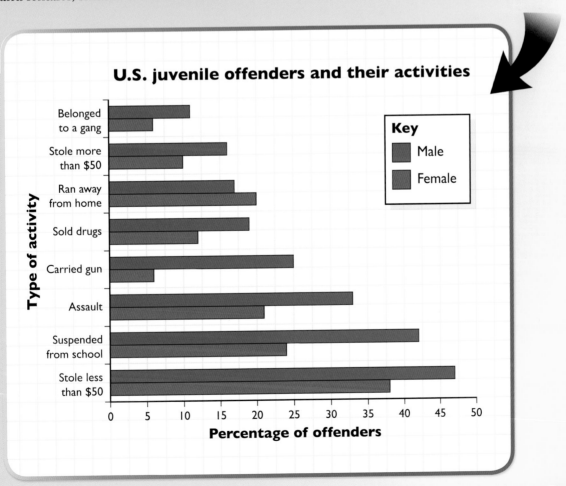

GLOSSARY

arson criminal act of deliberately starting a fire

assault act of causing bodily harm to another person

cell unit or group

community service unpaid work that benefits the community, such as working for a charity

court place where a trial takes place

criminal person who has committed a crime

Crown Court court where trials for serious crimes, such as murder, are held

defence case presented on behalf of an accused criminal

defendant accused person in a trial

detective police officer who investigates and solves crimes

enforce make someone follow the law

evidence facts available that prove guilt or innocence of a crime

felony serious crime

fraud deceptive plan to gain money

grand jury group of people called to decide if a serious crime has been committed and whether the person accused should stand trial

guilty responsible for committing a crime

hit-and-run situation in which a driver strikes a person with his or her car and flees the scene of the accident

homicide taking of a human life

identification documents that prove a person is who he or she claims to be

illegal against the law

innocent found to not have committed a crime

international among several countries

invest putting money to use to earn more money, such as through buying stocks or real estate

jury group of people who decide on evidence in a trial

justice fair treatment

juvenile person below adult age

local police officer who works for a city or town government

manslaughter crime of killing a human being without prior planning

misdemeanour minor crime

money laundering investing illegally earned money to make it difficult to trace

murder deliberate taking of a human life

offender person who commits a crime

parole release of a prisoner, depending on good behaviour

premeditated planned in advance

prison building in which people are held as punishment for crimes

probation release from detention, depending on good behaviour

prosecution side of a trial that presents the case against the accused

punishment imposing a penalty as payment for committing a crime

sentence period of time a criminal must spend in prison

summary minor or petty crime

terrorism use of violence and fear for political or religious aims

trafficking dealing or trading in illegal items

trial formal test of evidence in a crime to determine whether a person is guilty or not

victim person harmed or injured

white-collar working in a professional job

x-axis horizontal line on a graph

y-axis vertical line on a graph

FURTHER INFORMATION

Books

Britain: the Facts: Law and Order, Christopher Riches (Franklin Watts, 2008)

Crime and Detection, Brian Lane and Laura Buller (Dorling Kindersley, 2005)

Crime Scene Detective, Carey Scott (Dorling Kindersley, 2007)

Crimebusters, Clive Gifford (OUP, 2007)

Issues in Our World: Terrorism, Ewan Mcleish (Franklin Watts, 2007)

Solve It With Science (series) (Franklin Watts, 2009)

True Crime: Crime Scenes, John Townsend (Raintree, 2004)

Websites

This site provides information about various types of crime. It also gives tips on how to stay safe.
http://www.direct.gov.uk/en/YoungPeople/CrimeAndJustice/index.htm

Ideas on this site combine efforts by both adults and children in fighting gun and knife crime.
http://www.11million.org.uk/adult/gun_and_knife_crime/

Learn about final warnings and test your memory on this site.
http://www.cleveland.police.uk/kids

INDEX